IN SEARCH OF
THE LOTUS FEET

IN SEARCH OF THE LOTUS FEET

ARUP MITRA

ATLANTIC
PUBLISHERS & DISTRIBUTORS

Published by
ATLANTIC PUBLISHERS AND DISTRIBUTORS
B-2, Vishal Enclave, Opp. Rajouri Garden, New Delhi-27
Phones : 5413460, 5429987, 5466842

Sales Office
4215/1, Ansari Road, Darya Ganj, New Delhi-110 002
Phones : 3273880, 3285873, 3280451
Fax : 91-11-3285873
web : www.atlanticbooks.com
e-mail : info@atlanticbooks.com

ISBN 81-269-0175-6

Typeset at
APD Computer Graphics, Delhi

Printed in India at
Nice Printing Press, Delhi

...at the lotus feet

REVIEWER'S REPORT

Reading the heart-touching poems penned down by Mr. Arup Mitra has been an unusual experience for me. Most of the poems highlight the spiritual yearning of the poet. In search of the Divine Truth, the poems are an expression of the poet's subconscious thoughts.

It is interesting to note the poet's creativity as he personifies lotus in several of his poems and uses the humble flower to express his inner desires.

The poesy contains three sections. While the first two parts define the poet's feelings towards God, in the third part, the poet vents his anger against the exploitation of the have-nots by the rich people.

I would be happy to recommend this work for publication.

ACKNOWLEDGMENT

Though authors, as Somerset Maughum writes, are touchy about their productions and inclined to resent unfavorable criticism they are wretchedly aware of their limitations and seldom satisfied with their own work. Hence, it is the encouragement that, one receives from friends and readers, helps sustain the creativity of the mind. I am grateful to all who inspired me after reading "Awakening" to publish another volume of poems.

Thanks are due to Ms. Vandana Preyashi for her generous editorial support. I would like to express my gratitude to my teachers in school, who kindly led the right direction to my "spontaneous overflow of emotions recollected in tranquility."

ARUP MITRA

CONTENTS

PART I

LOOKING BEYOND THE HORIZON

PART II

WAVES OF JOY

PART III

AGAINST THE DISHONOUR

PART I

Looking beyond the horizon

GODDESS OF WISDOM

Emptiness of the space
Contains the waves of
Knowledge, music and peace –
The manifestation of the endlessness
Of the Goddess of wisdom;
Human mind catches the vibrations
As it rests in equanimity,
In bliss;
And through the rigor of life
They take the physical form,
From the depth of wordlessness
Is born the beauty of expressions.

Forgetfulness of the human mind
About the supreme links
And the source of energy,
Nurtures the ego,
And the self claims its right
Over what does not belong to him –
For nothing can be in possession of a machine
Which can only operate
Under instructions
Flowing in the garb of invisibility.

The constant struggle
Of the self
To prove its absolute existence

Breeding infinite forces
Of destruction
Is on;
They arise with vigor to chase away the
Creative forces
And fall back on them unsuccessfully,
In the process creating frictions
Within the self –
And the personality
Looks distressed,
More so in confusion;
Nevertheless one bow of surrender
With love
Sets him free from the chains of torture
As the mind resumes its flight
In the eternal space –
In pursuit of the Goddess of wisdom.

★ ★ ★

YOU: A MODERN ART

Half-understood and multi-faceted,
Unfolding the reality
That can be viewed
From all possible angles –
Simple as well as Complex;
Wide variations in life
Reflected in perceptions and ways of admiration
Are compiled in one format
Demonstrating the compatibility among differences;

Truth and falsehood
Contained in the same container
Suggesting in absolute sense
Nothing is good or bad –
Two can dwell in one personality
Playing hide and seek with each other–
The cause to die
Can also be the cause to live.

***

MY TURN

When you gave me your flute
I played upon it not,
Frittered the grace.
Today when you take my flute in your hands
And fill it with ethereal rhythm
I feel restless and brood over the past,
I wish, I had soothed your ears when it was my turn.

The dark clouds of rainy July
Appear over and over again
Casting your shadow on my mind's eye
Beside my physical form–
I peer above the eucalyptus trees
To see if your eyes behold mine.

I run behind the butterflies to reach the blossoms,
Place my ears on their petals
To hear the silent vibrations of your unseen footsteps.

★ ★ ★

BODOBURU TEMPLE

From the heart of the stone
Expressions of compassion
Flow like a many-headed fountain–
Thou art seated on a lotus posture,
Or standing somewhere with your hands
Extended to offer
The greatest gift to the world
Rotting in misery and passion.

Time could not wash away
The grace of your presence
That the skilful hands could successfully curve
While raising your statue,
Rains and the sun left deep marks on your body,
Religious intolerance and invasion
Left you beheaded and deformed,
Yet, from the heart of the stone
A voice says, 'Om manipadme hom,'
From the ruins of history echoes
The immortal message of kindness
For those unkind mortals,
Who cannot live
And let others live in peace.

★★★

VICTORY

Stand within the range of my sight
I would need to look up to you when my might
Would claim for a share in your free world –
I would like to be struck deeply by your sword.

Remain in front of my eyes
So that in distress and joy I realize
Your love is flowing over my body and soul
To raise me high above all.

Play with me the game of hide and seek
To remove the spell of the clouds thick,
After the exhaustion of a long seeking
In the peace of satiety let me sink.

Let your chariot stand in the southern breeze
As my existence comes to cease,
Blow your conch shell louder and louder
To signify your success that over me you shower.

★ ★ ★

AMBITION

My ambition is sky high –
One tiny flower I offer you
I expect,
Would fetch me all your love
And unravel your endlessness.
Your universal form
Can help me fight all superstition,
Which mind has gathered
In the name of religion
Mind has gathered over the centuries.

One little drop of tear I shed
Seeing the cranes fly in the sky –
Dark clouds in the background –
I want to pour all your music
In this flute of my life –
Help me create immortality
From each of these mortal movements.

★★★

DROP BY DROP

I have got to gather
Love for you,
My lord!
I always have thought,
When you would appear,
I will dig up an ocean
Overnight in my heart;
But my days I spend
Playing the sport of pleasure,
My action can only fetch
Fame and wealth.

Stars flicker,
The sun grimes,
The greenery mocks,
And I die in shame–
Standing on a vast stretch of sand
I offer you only a mirage
Instead of an oasis
That I promised you my lord!

☆ ☆ ☆

LONGING

If tears have beautified my love
Like a lotus with dew drops on its petals,
Like the silhouette of the ridge
After the heavy downpour of July,
If my love has spreads its sweetness
Like the fragrance of the wet jasmine
Why does not the boat stop at my shore
To respond to my age-old call?

My earthen urn is beneath the water,
I gently pull it up –
It moves smoothly
As long as it is below the level,
With difficulty then
I lift it up on my head
And watch my every step
On my return journey –
Tomorrow I will have to come back here
And try my luck again.

★★★

REVENUE

A lone lotus in the centre of a lake
Reminds me of life –
A tiny island
Amidst the vast ocean,
Which day by day
Tries to swallow the land.
Yet I cultivate
More and more,
Through my action,
The piece of land I have got in my possession.
I illumine it
For, I know, it can be my only gift to the world,
Which the world will preserve
In her immortal hands,
But I have got to detach myself
From this gift too
For, I have to pay my little self to death
As revenue of the land
That I have enjoyed
All through my life.

★ ★ ★

MY LAST BUYER

I keep returning from market to market
With a heavy load on my back,
In search of a suitable customer
I have spent from dawn to dusk;

I wish, I had given up the hope
Long before I was tired,
I would not then have had the pain
Of not being hired;

I cannot succumb to defeat,
Or do you think I possibly can –
I have always felt like bursting into tears
In the face of the storm when I ran.

My journey from non-manifested to manifested,
And the return path between the two
If all have already been made so evident
For the sale, alas, why didn't I turn to you?

★★★

A CRIMINAL'S VOICE

Thou are the creator
And thou ask me why!
Why did I perform this?
Didn't you yourself implant it in my nature
In my very self when you generated me?

Then you said,
The nature is an outcome of action
Of mine or of my predecessors –
Every action would have its
Equal and opposite reaction –
It's only a matter of time.

I wish
I had utilized the power I had
To try and suppress my propensities,
Worked hard to ignite the lamp of love,
That lay in the dark corner of my heart,
My present action
Would have then salvaged
What it remained implanted in my nature,
And I would have then been saved
From the plethora of my action that ran mad.
These outcomes would not then have appeared at all,
I would have been a different creature,
But the inner voice was not loud enough
To cross the boundary of what is bad.

★ ★ ★

THE HIDDEN GEM

Penetrating the layers of winds,
The sounds and their echoes,
Can the music of my prayer
Reach the ocean of silence you dwell in?

From the basket of flowers can those
I chose to offer you at your altar
Convey you that my heart transformed
Into a complete lotus in the process?

Will the list of my visitors I entertain
With smiles, tears and regards
Be sufficiently large to include at last
The name of the stranger that I look for?

The happiness that twinkles in my sorrow and pleasure
Perhaps cannot contain the fragrance of your garland,
It only reminds me of my unfinished task
That you had assigned me on your job on the earth.

★★★

ETERNAL SEEKING

I keep unfolding the petals of the lotus
One after another,
One planet after another,
One solar system after another,
One milky path after another,
Till it is in full bloom at your feet.

You touch my every nerve
Through my sorrow and joy
Through my turmoil and peace
Through all my experience
Till I become the fragrance
Of your most desired lotus.

Your efforts and my seeking
Are eternal
Hope keeps them going –
One day we would converge.
And the day we converge
Existence ends
Hope only keeps them going
Eternally.

* * *

IN EXCHANGE OF MY SATISFACTION

You and I
Were traveling in your sky,
We happened to cross
The orbit of the earth –
The dawn was about to set in
The red glow was only faintly visible
Like a brook
On the mountain range of royal blue ether-
Power was shining
On the forehead of knowledge.

My eyes fell on those
White jasmine
Scattered all around
In the courtyard of a small cottage.

I insisted we stop for a while
To decorate myself
With bouquets and garlands
To the best of my satisfaction.

Seeing my keenness you reminded me
Of the price that I would have to pay
It could be enormous –

Because every acceptance involves an exchange.

I was adamant
For, my heart was captured
By those charming little buds -
I took no note of your advice.

As I descended
The go of the earth
Imprisoned me
In her intricate games
Following endlessly
One after another
Causally linked to each other,
And there is no solution
To this simultaneous system.

I wept-
Begged of you
Not to leave me-
Your consort-
But you obeyed sincerely the rules
That you once framed yourself
For everyone,
And for yourself too.

In my effort
To keep my memory alive
That I belong to you-
The center of the universe-
My services I promise to offer
To all creatures on the earth,
My love for you I pour
In the candle I light every night;

You have promised
To break open all my chains
And release me someday
Into your eternal sky,
Before that you would of course
Test my patience,
My faith
In all possible ways;
If I fail
I will have to play the game again,
Starting from the scratch.

★ ★ ★

HOPE

Even god cannot eliminate the evil–
The destructive force is
Always stronger than its counterpart
He can only give strength
To withstand the attack of the evil,
In the process of struggle
One has to incur
A great deal of loss.
The only hope is that
God would see through
The enticing phase of the evil
And one would continue to exist
Even when the evil has done its part–
Of course the existence need not be defined
On the physical plane alone.

This thin ray of hope
Has unfolded several
Blossoms of imagination
In the human mind
Over the ages
And men have
Overestimated
The power of God,
But this is what
Sustained the human confidence,
Almost assuring immortality.

Evil does not die
For it cannot die,
It is as immortal as
Its counterpart,
It can only be suppressed
But only to an extent
With countless efforts
And strife–
The last glow of the setting run
Leaves the hope
Of seeing the rising sun
Once again the next morning.

★★★

BIASES

Controversies
About truth exist
For we can know only a tiny fragment of it
And cling to it
The rest of our lives,
Casting evidence in its favour only,
The tiny fragment is
Believed to represent the whole.
Biases
Which the mind inherits and absorbs
Get further substantiated
By evidence-
For we record only
What suits us,
And ignore what does not.

Differences in fragments
Get translated into
Differences in opinions
And the politics of
Knowledge continues,
From generation to generation,
While you joyfully
Manage to hide yourself
From the human mind.

☆ ☆ ☆

FROM MYSTICISM TO EXISTENCE

In my world I have your statue
Which I decorate with flowers and fragrance
All through my life
I imagine your features
And expect a sudden appearance.

In your world you are almighty
And I am merely a lotus
Placed at your feet
At your hands
At your neck
But depending upon my choice,

In my world as I work
According to my wish
I cause loss
To myself and to the world,
But as I work having you as the ultimate doer
Creativity follows
Enormously,
As seeking gains strength and vigor
Your world and my world converge
To overcome the process of destruction –
The net result is existence.

★★★

MY BROKEN PUPPET

A broken puppet I gave you in return
As you stood beyond the candle light
And beyond the stars of the milky path
To shower your blossoms of the music
In the dry desert sand of the earth
Only a broken puppet I gave you in return.
I said, 'it is you'
I said, 'it symbolises you'-
All ended in confusion.

Today as I open my cottage door
To witness the universal tree
Lying on an ever integrated plane
Of what are past, present and future for me
I find the toy in the best of its colour
Riding one of the branches
Endowed with new leaves
I cry out to reach my puppet
I want it, 'give it to me at any cost'-
In search of the puppet my struggle begins
In the light and darkness,
Closing my eyes desperately
I pull myself in like a tortoise
I seek it within me,
I want my broken puppet at any cost!

★ ★ ★

THE BLUE BIRD

All the birds had arrived
In the festival of spring,
Only the blue bird was missing
Every one cried, "without him there is no charm."

In search of the blue bird
Messengers ran to all forests and sky,
Ages passed, no one returned
The world started puffing in tension.

Men initiated killing each other,
Every one blaming everyone
For the disappearance of the bird
Chaos was let loose
And as the people roared
The blue bird decided to
Fade away further in fear.

It faded away into the depth of the blue sky,
Into the depth of the gloom of the mind,
In hallucination people cried, and then became silent again,
In solitude they discovered the blue bird at once.

★★★

THE CHAIN OF CONTINUITY

Among the human beings
While being one of them
You are dressed in
Gorgeous colours,
Jewelry and gems,
You suffer illness
And experience joy,
You desire to see your dear ones,
You seek love,
You at times act obstinately
Like a child,
And you get angry too.
Then you cease to take on the human form,
With a great force
And power your appear
In super human form,
Removing obstacles for others
And granting their prayers
For self-improvement –
Through knowledge, action, purity and peace.
And sometimes in no definite shape
Just a piece of stone perhaps
Emitting the rays of equanimity,
Then you express yourself
As a thin ray of light,
Firm yet almost invisible
And then in

The atom and the nucleus-
The invisible strength-
From all forms you disappear
To appear formlessness,
Stronger the power grows
Finer and more invisible you become
And finally an infinite consciousness
Within which dwell and which dwells in
All living beings and non-living objects too,
All in the process of transformation-
From matter to consciousness
You are the content and the container too-
You are the ever evolving spirit
In constancy and changelessness.
A great mass of energy,
Manifested through a point
Spread out in the whole universe.
A chain of continuity
Connecting all grades, planes and spaces;
Including all that remains excluded
By the standard set by senses.

★★★

COMPROMISE

I heard the footsteps
In my slumber
I asked in delirium,
"Who are you!"
A voice replied,
"I have come to see you."
In my half chocked voice with emotion
I asked again, "Where are you?"
Hands touched my forehead
And I remember,
Each of the fingers was like a lotus
I tried hard to look but couldn't.
Something was trying hard
To put me into the lull
And my consciousness struggled
To see the Kindness
In its physical form.
In this struggle
My entire life I spent
At last arriving at a compromise:
To utter your name
Half-asleep.

★ ★ ★

THE WINTER TREE

The under-current flows in me–
Not dead, I am alive;
Winter has shaken me from the core –
Taken away all my leaves.
Yet, misery could not touch my soul –
The rhythm runs in every pore
From ruins of the past
I hope to build the palace
On the path of eternity
With serenity
That misery has taught.

★ ★ ★

THE INVISIBLE FACE

You hold for me in your eyes
The beauty of flowers
Steeped in the pain of separation
Yet, giving out the fragrance of a secret-union.
In the ocean of life you are void
But not empty,
You are immobile
But witness all my agility
From one infinity to another,
You hold for me the fruits
Of all my struggle
Which, I think, have gone in vain.

⭑ ⭑ ⭑

BETWEEN MY EGO AND LOVE

I ask for your grace,
To conceal
Your assistance,
That I receive
In enriching me
Day by day;
And may tell the world,
All my intelligence
Has come through
My efforts alone,
And I may keep up
The arrogance of my little self.

My prayers have found
Shelter in your mercy–
Your generous hands have poured
In me enormously
Without trying to judge
My worthiness.

I beg of you today
To stand firm
Between my ego and love –
Let not the dim light of the candle
Appear invisible
Due to the gorgeous lights of the street.

☆☆☆

BEHIND YOUR INFINITENESS

Don't you think, my lord
You will be able to hide yourself
From me.
You forget,
My mind contains
Both your forms:
Of vastness and finiteness,
I will follow you in the milky-path
Holding the garland,
I carry from the earth;
Your chariot moves ahead,
But you turn back to see me
For, my love is pulling you behind.
You cannot hide your finite form
Behind your infiniteness.

★ ★ ★

SOIL SAYS

Let me have the pleasure
Of earning my livelihood
In exchange of my perseverance
So that at the dusk of my life
I may present you
The garland of my immense recollections
Of my strife, tears and love.

Let me not have the pleasure
Of enjoying my leisure lazily,
And earn a bad name
Of having wasted the resources
Like the spoilt child
Of a wealthy father.

***

LORD OF THE RUINED TEMPLE

Oh the lord of the ruined temple!
I worship you when no one else in the neighborhood
Recognises you,
I bow to you
When you are treated
By others
As a mere piece of stone,
Or a toy.
Oh the lord of the ruined temple!
I adore you
And dare to offer you my love
In moments of pitch darkness.
Tomorrow your temple
Will take a new shape -
Lights will glow
All along the walls,
The deity will dazzle
In jewelry and gems
And there will be
A long queue of devotees
At the temple gate,
I will not be there
For, I would have left
For my longest journey
In search of you.
But would you then
Look for me

In the crowd
And recall,
It was me who had brought
The first offerings
Oh the lord of the ruined temple!

* * *

EMPTY ME TILL I'M FULL

Let all my light of hope
Welcome you,
You only,
Shattering the sky-high
Ambitions of my immature mind
Let not achievements
Which I have taken in ignorance
As completion of life
Create illusions any more;
In the music of destruction
Let me hear your rhythm
Of unending creativity.
Empty me
Till I realize,
I am full to the brim
With your joy –
Your joy alone.

☆☆☆

NOT IMAGINATION ONLY

The evening star
Looks bright
Darkness is filtered with light
Before it bids the final good-bye,
I bend down
From the half-opened window
Of my life,
No, it has to be you
Who sets his foot out,
From the chariot,
I can see
Your beauty,
Your magnificent glamour –
In the trees,
In the mountain range,
In the milky-path
And in the ocean
You cannot
Be an imagination,
You are the truth
Of the senses,
Beyond the senses.

★★★

THE MIND OF GOD

His mind is set free
From his own control
To follow the rules of nature
Which in the process of creation evolved,
Man is empowered
To carry the potentiality
To change as he wants –
Man's thoughtful action,
Sincerest prayers
Can bring what is subtle and silent
To the fore
And utilize the energy
As he pleases
For, He has left it to man generously.
It can be used
In constructive or destructive pursuits
Depending upon man's wishes –
Both co-exist
One manifested,
Another not manifested,
Interchangeably.
Human mind, matter and moment –
Outcomes of God's mind –
Travel to set in the dusk of god's mind.

☆ ☆ ☆

IGNORANCE

I realize not
Your enormous strength–
The suns and planets
Are tied in your garland.
But I call you my friend,
I treat you a part of my household,
I feel proud of my offerings
Knowing hardly that
You are beyond
My perception.
I derive satisfaction
To have offered you a seat
In the middle of hundred petals
Of the lotus of my heart,
From the inner shrine
Of my life.
You must have
Laughed at my foolishness.

★★★

SLUGGISH PROGRESS

The stream of words
And the stream of ideas
Flow on the opposite poles:
Which one should I take
To row my boat on
To reach the ocean?
The former looks more graceful,
Flows smoothly
Hindering not the progress
But its cyclical nature
Brings one back to
From where the journey began.
The latter is rough
So, progress is sluggish,
But it looks not behind
Weeps not for
What has been left on the shore,
It crosses the horizon
To travel further down,
The golden sun and the silver moon –
None can alter its flow.
The vast stretch of water
Spreads limitlessly,
Into the bottomless ocean
Which opens up in search of the unknown.

☆☆☆

WINNING YOU

I ask for your blessings
To help me get
Wealth, fame and power –
I wish to stand
On top of the world.
My prayers are granted
I wonder then how could you
To help me attain
What are merely transient
Spend your precious energies?

I think, I may awake
To look beyond my horizon
But in the depth of my wishes
I remain immersed eternally–
One begets hundreds
And then multiply every second
Into countless number
Leading me to an ocean
From where I can never come out in my life –
Another life I require –
But now desires are born again
And thus the perpetual journey is on.
You derive immense pleasure
From my journey of eternity.
Somewhere beneath this soft sand
You have fixed your rope –

If only I could reach
I would be out
And your game would be over.
You struggle hard
To hide the rope
Putting in its place
Generous gifts of pleasure.
But if I take my hands off,
And break into tears
Remembering you desperately
Will you then keep your heart steady?
Doesn't matter if I know a little of all
But a great deal of none,
I wait for the moment
When I would value you more
Than all that I have acquired
Or aspired to acquire.

★ ★ ★

MISER

The lord asked the devotee
For his contribution,
The devotee
Touched his wallet,
Stepped back,
Recollected,
He did not have
Any small change to offer,
The large amounts
Are not meant for
Such purposes,
On his return
The devotee discovers
Small changes in his purse
"Where do they come from?"
"Oh, yes!" He recalls, "I always had them."
Did it slip his mind?
Or the fear
That he might have to take out larger amounts
In case he didn't find any small change,
Made him forgetful!
It's too late,
The lord has gone back.
Alas ! he could not offer
Which he could afford
Willingly and joyously
In trying to save the larger amounts,
Desperately,
Uselessly.

★ ★ ★

BEYOND BARTER

You reminded me that
I promised you a sacrifice
When you granted me my wish
Which with great intensity I had prayed for.
I thought it was a mere coincidence,
Things were to work out in my favour after all,
Prayers have nothing to do with the positive effects –
I need not be superstitious,
And ignored your reminder.
As the boat entered the deep sea
Clouds covered the sky from all sides,
I prayed to you again,
And promised lofty
Gifts in return,
You smilingly protected me
And reminded again of my promises,
But I know not what struck my mind again
And I ignored all, taking it to be my superstition;
Today I realize, it was you
Who created this illusion in me
So that I could come out of
The give and take principle,
And offer you my unconditional love.

★ ★ ★

IMPATIENCE

Every night I decorated the room
And lit the lamp enthusiastically,
But every morning I woke up sadly
To find that lord never visited my altar.
The sandal wood paste
And the garland dried up
Wasting their fragrance,
Drops of tears stopped losing their coarse
In the rocks and sand of hopelessness.
One night when I cared not
To keep the plate of worship ready,
When I sang not your praises,
And filled not the room with light and smell,
Your foot steps I heard –
They came closer and woke me –
I have nothing to offer you, my lord
In dark,
"How could I do this?" I curse myself,
I wish I only had a little hope and patience
To keep up my love for you in me.

★★★

SAVIOR'S WORRY

Sin and sinners have flooded the world
The lord must burn them
After the virtuous ones are elevated
To merge with the lord,
The savior wonders
Looking at the deep blue sky
Who would tell him,
"I love you,"
And express the eternal joy,
Who would bring him the scented flowers
In folded hands
And tell him, "Save me lord!"
Save me from my futile efforts
To recreate myself
Dismissing your contribution in my life?

Idly looking at the stars
You would lament for the spring
You would miss
The music that the waves of the ocean
Pour into the human voice,
No, both the sin and virtue
Must co-exist
Without one the other cannot survive,
And if nothing remains
Your heart would break in pain.

★ ★ ★

PART II
Waves of joy

PEBBLE BEACH

What game do you plan to play today
With the rainbow in your hands,
When you stand above the ocean of Pacific?

The breeze carries your words into my ears
And the waves add music to them,
I sing to you the notes of your praise
While the sky looks deep into my eyes.

Oh the source of all-knowledge
What charming form you possess!
All my love is awakened like the waves –
And the light has penetrated
The dark dungeon of my heart.

★★★

BARTER

Thousands of candles of my sorrow and joy
Are lit to welcome you into my life,
You who have numerous stars in your evening sky
Make your presence feel in depths of darkness.

I try to hold my body, mind and soul together
To offer you a complete lotus,
The contents of your garland for me
Contains the tiny grass leaf to millions of suns in the milky path.

In my finite form lies the infinite imagination
I can stretch from one infinity to another
I can captivate your heart from the gloom of emptiness
And make you mingle with my every breath.

★ ★ ★

ETERNAL MUSIC

Death and destruction
Disturb the creativity of mind
Only temporarily,
The music that you have poured
In human mind
Is unending;
The external music
Reawakens the inner one,
And carries the mind away
Into the depth of silence,
Above the waves of disturbance;
There is misery,
There are worries, haunting life ceaselessly,
But life offers your blessings too
In the form of eternal music.

★★★

POETRY IN YOU

Blossoms of scattered thoughts
With fragrance of depth
Are tied in an unbroken thread
To offer a meaning to life –

Patches of clouds
Gathering to raise the density,
With the drops of rains
They create a new dimension for life –

Little candles are put together
To illumine the entire sky,
On the forehead of darkness they dazzle
To portray the completeness of life.

★ ★ ★

INDIFFERENCE

Little by little you captured my heart
When I was longing for a mate
With all luxury around,
In non-realization of my
Wishful thinking
Lay your victory,
Progressing steadily
Without my knowledge.

Today when the world opens up
To offer more than what my hands can hold
In my entire life,
The heart refuses –
Expresses indifference
For all I had once longed,
In the darkness of ignorance
Who knew,
The glow of light was taking shape!
Who knew,
The banner of your victory
Was raising its head
Little by little on the top of the mountain of
What I thought were my failures.

★ ★ ★

INACTION

Keep all the work aside –
The rains of July have poured
An intoxication on the earth –
Let the mind escape into the eternal sky today.

Let the song of the soul
Mingle with the chirping of the birds
Let the eyelids move uninterrupted
Like the leaves in the moist wind.

Let the flute be played upon
Inside the dense bushes where peacocks dance,
Let the doors of the cell be unlocked
To set the prisoners and the misers free.
Let the mind be alone today,
And the silence of the leisure soothe
The fathoms of words to say,
"Peace, Peace, Peace–
In every atom of the existence
let it mix!"

★★★

EQUILIBRIUM

Life–
A series of equilibrium,
There's a constant struggle
To move from
One equilibrium to another,
From lower to higher
Level of acquisition
The forces that disturb equilibrium
Are stronger and more powerful
Than the forces that work
Towards attaining equilibrium,
What is perceived, therefore,
Is only a continuous state of disequilibrium
Or multiple disequilibria,

But the mechanism –
The determination –
Implanted in the system
To return to equilibrium
Is strongest of all;
Sorrow and suffering
That is why remain
Beneath the feet of life,
They cannot win over life–
The chariot of life has
Conquered them all –
In its eternal pursuit
To attain the highest level of equilibrium.

★★★

FROM WORK TO SILENCE

Your chariot would cross my cottage door!
The excitement has kept me awake,
Night after night I watch the stars
And pass my days dreaming.

Your plentiful hands would give me
All I have imagined in my life
Lists of my golden wishes
I keep making all the time.

At last your golden chariot
Has come to a halt at my door step
I stand spell-bound with a garland in my hand
Dropping half into the dust.

Where are my wishes and words gone!
What charm have you cast on me!
I stand like a lifeless statue –
Only my eyes burst into tears.

Such is your wish that
When I get the chance
I won't be able to ask you for
What I have always desired;

Your wishes you would pour in me –
The light of your lamp would light mine –
I am just a pool of water to grow
Lotuses for you when you need.

★★★

LIGHT OF SIN

I knew not
Who left a cherry for me
While I was completely engrossed,
Listening to the chirping of birds
With the leaves between my fingers
The sky I was trying to hold.

The earth shook with great vigor
And my body collapsed
As soon as the pill of temptation
I swallowed.

The dimension of mind changed
I was reborn to know you better
My energy was at once restored,
From the depth of darkness
screamed, I could see the light,
Your un-spelt words I have followed.

★★★

CONSCIOUSNESS

Thou art seated on a lotus
In the lotus posture
Holding a lotus in your hands,
A garland of lotus hangs around your neck,
Thou art the lotus in the midst of one million lotus.

Joy, peace and kindness
Flow from your face
Jewels of ethereal glory shine on your crown
Prosperity that leads to renunciation and perfection
Rolls generously beneath your feet.

From nothingness to existence and *vice versa*
Your action spreads to bestow completion.

★ ★ ★

NOTHINGNESS

From the depths of nothingness
The golden harp transmits its rhythm
To each of the veins of the lotus with thousand petals,
And thus flows the music in its physical form.

The vibrations of the music
Help bloom the lotus and spread all its petals,
Which then transcends the physical form
Into the space of nothingness.

The rocks melt and vegetation wilts
To merge into nothingness,
Equanimity emerges ceaselessly,
Peace prevailing in stillness.

★★★

RED, YELLOW AND WHITE

The boat is ready to set out–
Three stretches of water it has to cross –
The red sea, yellow sea and white sea –
At the end the land of peace is believed to exist.

Three curtains lie on my mind–
The red, yellow and the white
And I try to remove them quickly,
Little by little they disappear.

The vibrations of an unsung music
I expect to follow at the end of my song
Which I offer to you with a bunch of flowers
Of three shades – the red, yellow and white.

Angels chant no more your praises
Nor devils perform the dance of destruction
Your touchstone you have placed in that land
Transforms all into jewels invaluable.

★ ★ ★

NO RESIDUE

I keep gazing at you,
Thinking that you would speak
To let me know
That my wishes have been granted
Which I store in the softest corner of my mind.

The light from your candle
Enters my thoughts unknowingly
And ignites the base
On which my desires rest
I stand before thee silently
Clinging to the painful pleasure to its last drop,
And then when my turn comes
You smilingly ask me
To spell out all my wishes,

I find there is no residue left,
You have removed them all
Before they could be granted.
I bow to you –
Word have lost themselves in you.
People call it death but the silent voice rings
"Love, it is all love,
It is the Heavenly love."

★★★

CHANGELESSNESS

The decay of one sun
Is accompanied by the
Creation of another
The net result is changelessness
There is no absolute death, or life
All is relative –
In the long run we are all constant.
Your chariot is in continuous motion
For the candles are forever burning
To welcome your arrival
In numerous earths
All around the cosmos –
There is neither any beginning
Nor an end
Of what exists.

★★★

THE FIRST SPRING

At my southern door
You stand, my love
Tell me how to greet you in joy?

My eyes look into your eyes,
My mind on the red
Border of your feet,
A handful of buds is all
I have got to offer you,
Tell me how to greet you in joy?

The candle of my life
I hold near your forehead
And make you sit
On the throne of my death,
Let the southern breeze
Unravel your guise
And pour fragrance on your tender frame,
While I try to count the falling leaves.

★★★

ON ATTAINING GOD

On attaining god
Can man start flying?
Or build castles on the ocean?
Can he convert stones into human beings
And trees into animals?
Miracles–
Even if they are true
Cannot comprise what is invaluable,
Perhaps, to strengthen faith
Some demonstrate
The unusual features,
On attaining god
Calmness follows,
The mind remains engrossed
In a bright glow of light
Like the mid-day sun,
But cool are the rays
As they are in the full-moon night.

* * *

ETERNAL QUESTION

I die in joy
To realize your kindness
Your own resources
You accept
In the form of my offerings to you
My heart is desperate to ask
In all my songs
In all my words,
In all my activities, smilingly and tearfully,
"Why be so gracious
To me, my Lord?"

Heart is overwhelmed
The feeling of full satisfaction
Rules over the mind –
Life is so complete.
The element of perpetuity
Blooms every moment
To make its presence felt
In every corner of my spirit
I die in joy and ask you again,
"Why be so gracious
To me, my Lord?"

☆ ☆ ☆

MAIDEN

After dipping herself in the river
Much before the dawn set in
She painted her floor in colours and flowers,
And set the lamps in every corner of her room
To wipe out darkness,
And welcome the first light of the day;
Drop of water on her hair
Like dew were falling on her forehead,
I asked her, "Maiden, whom do you wait for?"
She smiled and said, "My lord."
Before the evening set in
She again lit the candles at her door
Her hair was covered with *mallika* and *juhi*,
She was dressed in red and gold.
I asked her, "Whom do you wait for?"
She looked at me smilingly and said, "My lord."
In the depth of night she sat quietly
Dressed in yellow and white
Hardly opening her eyes or turning her face
She sat like a lotus motionless
I asked her again, "Maiden, whom do you wait for?"
She replied not, just gave a quick glance at me
"Self," she uttered not, only in gesture she explained,
A strange awe fell on me and I bowed to her.

* * *

CONFLUENCE

Today I realize
Your limitation,
Your difficulty,
In granting me
All my wishes,
Your inability to perform
All the miracles
Which I expected you to,
I realize, you too are
Bound by laws
That you created yourself
For yourself and everyone else
In the process of your creation.

Yet, I love you –
The lotus of my heart
Spreads its hundred petals
To offer you the purest seat
That I ever can offer,
And I realize
The confluence of
Your knowledge and love within me.

★ ★ ★

EARTH REPLIES

You question my rigidity!
You wonder why I prefer
Not to scatter myself
Over your world!
Cause you are just
Like the western wind
Of a stormy night –
I am aware
Of your ability
To raise every particle
From the earth
But all your pleasure
You can share
Is for fraction of a second only,
The fate of the bud
Which, in the temptation
Of flying in the air
Loses her floral chord,
Is rejection
Beneath the bush.
May I extend
All my tendrils
To hold to myself strongly
And swing in the morning breeze
Singing the ode of immortality,
Doesn't matter
If I could not fly high

And feel the depth of pleasure –
The stream of peace
That flows in me
Is steady, solemn and somber.

★★★

UNION

I was plucking the morning glory
And filling my empty basket,
As I suddenly turned around,
Oh! you in the eastern sky
With all your beams
Spreading over me
Over me,
Light -
The streams of light!
I stood blind for a while,
A total darkness
Enveloped my eyes;
Tears rolled down–
I sobbed and you smiled,
I know not
When you filled me
From within
As I lay dead
Beneath the bush.

⁂

REDEFINING YOU

My offerings, I estimate, are great
Because
I have learnt
To judge
From my point of view only.
You assess not
As per your standards
You value them more than I ever could.
At times I wonder,
My tears, garlands and candles,
Even what people call sincerity,
What importance do have
At the plane of abstraction,
Which is beyond all transactions:
Physical or meta-physical.
All that must have been to you
Like a bunch of games with puppets!
But it is a wonder
That you reserve the capability
To reciprocate more than proportionately
To whatever mode one chooses.
From ethereal to
What we call real
A constant transformation
Takes place
And you struggle hard
To appear in ever novel form

To accept all that one has to offer,
Even to an atheist you reciprocate
By encouraging him
To dismiss your existence.

⭑⭑⭑

TWO WORLDS

Two worlds of vastness
Separated by a point,
The bird roams around in one
From one eternity to another,
The strings of all experience
Draws to one direction
And one day all forces
Converge at a point-
Door to the other world of vastness
Opens at once -
What is the difference?
One has the physical presence
To justifying its existence,
The other does not,
It's compensated by
A non-physical existence
It has beauty
In its own way,
The stars and planets
All exist
Without physical body–
The commonality is,
The joy
Spreads its waves
In both the worlds of vastness.

★ ★ ★

FROM VEDAS TO THE VEDANTA

Without light
I won't exist,
Without air
I would cease,
Without water
I would die,
My fear drives me
To pray
To the lord of light,
To the lord of air,
To the lord of water,
And to many others,
I offer my respect, my salutation,
But my seeking doesn't stop
For, my love remains untapped
And the strength of that love
Breaks open the door
One night
To experience
The millions of sun,
Millions of galaxies
Millions of lords,
All resting in one arm,
The tears
Overflow
To realize that

The same arm surrounds me
It's not mere imagination,
It's the observation of the senses
Of the unobserved.

★ ★ ★

THE TEN GREAT KNOWLEDGE

From the process of destruction
As much as from
Creation and conservation,
From purity of beauty
As much as from the non-physical existence,
From prosperity and possession
As much as from sacrifice and renunciation,
From power and control
As much as from misery and helplessness,
From the sweetness of music
As much as from the dreadful sounds of horror
Emerge the images of ten great knowledge of the self
Offering completeness,
Rendering perfection,
And suggesting oneness in diversity.

☆ ☆ ☆

WHEN YOU DESCENDED IN HUMAN FORM

When you descended in human form
You remembered not your power
Which had made the Heaven dance
On earth,
You suffered the misery of a common being
You faced injustice patiently,
To justify your intense love for truth,
And casually let your body decay
In its human way
To assure the world
That truth is immortal.
It lies much beyond the
Domains of mere physical existence,
The couple engaged in inter-course
And remain beneath your feet,
You stard high above the world of affairs
Holding your
Self-slaughtered head in one hand
And the sword of knowledge in the other,
The stream of blood
Shoots up like a fountain
From your neck,
One part enters your own mouth
Symbolizing your indestructibility,
And the other engages itself to please
The illusion that you have

Around you –
Truth is beyond
Existence and non-existence
Yet, manifested through them.

★★★

MOTHER

What beauty do you hold,
Mother!
My eyes I cannot turn away from you,
The red lotus at your feet
Keeps mesmerised all my senses.
The entire universe
Appears in your eyes;
In your kindness,
You transform
Yourself for my sake
Into the form
That my vision can withstand.
You are seen with your son in your arms -
In affection your eyes are half-closed,
You are seen near the lake
Engrossed in the music of your 'veena,'
You are seen on the hill
Meditating upon yourself,
You are visible in the garden
Decking your hair with blossoms,
Your kindness has no end;
You spread yourself in each atom
To transform the
Visible strength
Into invisible power
In the ocean of immortality.

★★★

THE AUSPICIOUS MOMENT

Yes, its significance is beyond imagination
For, it lies much above all calculations,
Much above all the measurements and comparisons
Of virtues and vices,
It's a moment
That reduces actions –
Good or bad –
Of millions of past lives
Into inaction –
All forgiven and forgotten –
Only I exist
Before your eyes
To witness love flowing from you
Into the inner self of mine,
Purifying my body and mind –
The steady light of the lamp
Glitters like the stars in the sky
The garland in my hands
I place at your feet
All the heavenly flowers –
The names that I don't know of –
Fill the air with your presence,
All that I aspired
But failed to spell out
Have now grown undesirable
Creating in the heart a complete satisfaction
And indifference that arise

After achieving them successfully,
No more apprehension in my self
About your decision on accepting me,
The moment that washes away the past,
The moment that ends the future
The moment that completes love
Is love itself.

★ ★ ★

PART III

Against the dishonour

BMW MURDER CASE

Arrogance of affluence
Manifests itself in
Parking the car at the wrong places,
Not applying the brake
When some one ordinary
Crosses the street
And comes incidentally
In the vicinity of the car –
The automobile has to keep moving.
They are fool to
Unnecessarily crowd the street,
They are there to die
For the smooth movement
Of the rich and the riches;
After all commodity is more precious
Than the human life;
What value do they have
When life begets life
Like germs and insects?
Well, at the most
Throw away a packet of
Currency notes
At those who resemble
The street dogs and cows,
They'll be satisfied
Rather overwhelmed
To get the valuables

In exchange of
Some valueless lives–
If a few were crushed
Among millions,
What difference does it make?
And to whom?
Rather it would help the nation
Eliminate her poverty–
Emotions of relatives!
Nonsense.
Some howling and crying!
All that will be settled in a few hours
And all in the household
Would start striving
For their livelihood.
And the State?
Oh it must strengthen those
Who bring riches for its
Smooth functioning–
Reciprocity is a must-
Useless to support the
Growth of liabilities–
Into this state of eternal freedom
A nation must march ahead!

★ ★ ★

AFTER THE STORM

Large limbs of palm and coconut
Were hanging in the air
Unfed children lying in the dust
Sobbing continuously,
While parents looked at the sky hopelessly.
Within a moment
What a great change has taken place?
Miserable are those
Whose misery ends never
And whom every whim of the nature
Is determined to affect more
Than the rest;
Miserable are those
Whose ignoble death gets no
Chants at the moment of cremation,
Miserable are those
Whose misery
Could make at least some people
Rich over night,
Empower them with wealth, status and power –
For next three generation at least
They do not have to struggle for bread,
Luxury, foreign trips
Coinciding with honeymoon,
And then false assurances to the society
Would overflow in the coming years
Making the existence of undeserving

More conspicuous and prominent
In the most important places
Which once happened to have given
Entry-pass to talent alone.
Thanks to misery and miserable,
Rich and riches can survive and grow,
Whatever the cost may be!

***

THE DISTRESS SALE

"Only for X you get two ma'am,
If you take four, I give X+Delta only."

"Can you make it four for X?"
The shrill voice poured in
From the rear seat
Without caring
To look into the
Hungry eyes of the seller
Outside the half-closed tanned glass
Of the window,
"That is below my sale price, ma'am."
"No, go away then."
"No, no ma'am please take them
But give me a little higher than what you said,
I can't survive that huge loss.
At the same time I must sell them, ma'am
Else I die, my family would die."
"No, shut up,
Don't speak unnecessary things."
"Have a heart ma'am
You can afford the price,
I can't bear the loss."
"Don't waste my time."

The starved faces of the children
Flash on the inner eye

It's the third consecutive day
He would have to return home without a pie;
Next consignment, he would
Have to pick up,
It's in the pipe line –
No money, order cancelled,
Someone else would be selected
For the commodity market to clear,
In a situation of unlimited supplies of labour
Who cares for what happens to an individual!
Looking at the soil
Feebly he says, "O.K. ma'am
Please take four for X."

The automobile started and picked up the speed
"You saw darling
Such a good buyer I am;
These lumpens keep such a big margin,
I got it for half the price.
These buggers need not ask for more,
These wretched street-sellers
Wasted so much of our time."
"And petrol of course,"
The voice from the rear seat added.

★ ★ ★

DEFINING TRUTH

As obstinate as a mule
He won't move his car an inch
He would not let the traffic pass,
He shouts at the cab driver
"You have hit me"
"No, I have not,
You came from the wrong side
And stood in front of me,
I have been trying to tell you
That you must let me pass"
"Shut up, I'll call the police"
"Call, then"
"You are at fault, gentleman,"
Says the passengers from the cab.
"You shut up, you need not intervene,"
Was the pat reply.
Police arrives and the man complains,
"The cab hit my car
These three –
The driver and the two passengers
Tried to hit me"
"Don't you feel ashamed
To utter such lies?"
Asked one of the passengers
"Thinking makes
Lie a lie, truth a truth,
It all depends how efficiently

You can manage the show,
For me, truth is what is convenient,
What majority can be made to believe,
Individual belief is a trash,
What only you believe to be truth
Is useless
Both to me and to you."

★★★

INAUSPICIOUS OFFERINGS

In exchange of her body
She has purchased the offerings
Quietly she proceeds
Towards the shrine
Looking downward –
Her mind full of fear
"Will they be acceptable?"
She wonders, for the priest knows her well –
He has come to her many a time.
Her heart
Palpitates at the feet of the lord,
"Accept my prayers and save my honour"
She murmurs as she crosses the threshold.

The priest looks at her
And growls in a hoarse voice
"How dare you come here?
Don't you understand,
Your shadow alone is sufficient
To pollute this place
Go away immediately,
Else heavens would fall on the head."

Both you and I were engaged
In the same act
Why aren't you considered inauspicious
If I am ?

Is it because
Your profession is different from mine,
But does profession
Hold any importance
Before God?
If so, then criminals,
Lawyers trying to save them
And many others of that kind
Ought to be penalized.
But they all are allowed to touch the deity
But not me.
I have not cheated anyone
But sold my body
To earn my livelihood.
It is my earning against which,
I have bought my offerings, like all others,
Why shouldn't they be acceptable to the lord?

"How dare you argue
And justify your activity?
Leave the place at once
You immoral female,
Don't you ever try to club me with you
You b——!"

The lady turns quietly,
Drops of tears fall on
The courtyard outside the temple door
As she wonders
"What do I do with these offerings!
Let me place them
At the root of this tree
In the name of the lord,

He is present everywhere, the omnipresent one,
He knows everything."

Flowers from the branches
Fell on her
As she got up after bowing down
"The Heavens have heard your call, lady
In the game of the three –
The priest, the deity and you –
You have won;
Both the priest and the idol
Look crazily
When the lord
Bends down from his chariot
To take you in his arms,
He has accepted
All you could offer."

★★★